HAPPY NATION?

HAPPY NATION?

Prospects for Psychological Prosperity in Ireland

Malcolm MacLachlan
and Karen Hand

The Liffey Press

Published by
The Liffey Press Ltd
Raheny Shopping Centre, Second Floor
Raheny, Dublin 5, Ireland
www.theliffeypress.com

© 2013 Malcolm MacLachlan and Karen Hand

A catalogue record of this book is
available from the British Library.

ISBN 978-1-908308-28-3

Printed in Ireland by Sprint Print.

CONTENTS

About the Authors

Malcolm 'Mac' MacLachlan is Professor of Psychology and Associate Director of the Centre for Global Health at Trinity College Dublin. He has worked as a clinical psychologist and as an organisational psychologist. He is a Fellow of the Psychological Society of Ireland and of the British Psychological Society, and a Member of the Royal Irish Academy.

Karen Hand is currently conducting PhD psychological research into branding and charities in the School of Psychology and Centre for Global Health at Trinity. She has worked extensively as a strategic communications planner and researcher in business and social sectors both internationally and in Ireland. She holds degrees in both business studies and psychology from Trinity College Dublin.

ACKNOWLEDGEMENTS

We would like to acknowledge the support of the School of Psychology and Centre for Global Health, Trinity College Dublin; the Science Gallery, Dublin City of Science and Vodafone in making the National Happiness Experiment a reality; RTÉ's John Murray and all of the media partners who helped spread the word and, most importantly, the 3,309 people in Ireland who participated in the experiment over the six weeks. We are also very grateful to David Hevey for his statistical expertise; Joanne McVeigh for her expert editorial assistance; to Francis Curran for the striking cover photograph and design; and to David Givens for The Liffey Press's professional and timely publication of this book.

ST. VINCENT DE PAUL

Fifty per cent of the authors' royalties for this book will be donated to St. Vincent de Paul to support their excellent work in supporting Irish society.

This book is dedicated to our major sources of happiness:

Anna-Helene, Tess, Lara and Eilish

and

Sarah, Zoe and Francis

PREFACE

Happiness? Surely not the stuff of a serious book – even a small one?!

Strange, that the very thing most people aspire to – to be happy – is somehow relegated to a thin psychological veneer, too elusive to understand, too 'simplistic' to study, too hedonistic to admit to wanting.

This short book presents an argument for psychological prosperity based on the results of the National Happiness Experiment conducted over the Summer of 2012 (we use the term 'summer' loosely). We combine some of the results from the National Happiness Experiment with the latest international research on happiness from around the world. We ask – how happy are we, and are we really willing to do what it takes to become happier?

The current crises spawned 'reset not a restart' rhetoric, but there are few signs of a fundamental rethink regarding what we should be 'set' for. The focus on economic expansion above all else has (ironically) back-fired economically and socially for Ireland and most of the Western world. This book outlines the health, social and psychological benefits of a society – and an economy – run 'as though people, and their happiness, mattered'.[1] The book is intended to be a focused argument, not an exhaustive review. We want to make frank and clear statements about what the evidence base on happiness suggests should be the policy imperatives for a nation seeking happiness. We will slay some dragons and pull the grass from under the feet of some sacred cows.

While we see this short book in the tradition of a Swiftian 'pamphlet', we don't see it as being 'party political', but rather 'people political'. So we don't present a critique of how our political parties align themselves, but rather issue a challenge to all of them – to identify just how they plan to implement the sort of actions that have a strong evidence-base to support their value in contributing to a happier nation. Like others, we believe that 'it's a shame to waste a good crisis'. Without taking a fundamental look at what is likely to make us happy, we will have no 'reset', only a coughing and spluttering restart, revving up until the next time the wheels fall off.

This year, 2012, marks 50 years of Psychology at Trinity College Dublin, and there have been various events to celebrate it, including the Happy? Exhibition at the Science Gallery and the National Happiness Experiment which followed it. The School's choice of these themes indicates a wish to engage with the mood of the nation, and to contribute to improving it. This volume wants to help set the country on a course which is likely to maximise what we call 'psychological prosperity', rather than – but not in opposition to – a purely financial prosperity.

People have assumed that having more 'stuff' would make them happier. In very poor countries, more 'stuff' can make a big difference: it can mean not being hungry, living in a safer environment, enjoying better health and better education. However, as countries become richer, 'more' really can mean 'less'. Most obviously, more food can mean being obese, being diabetic; and what is required to get 'more' can mean more stress, less coping and possibly more depression and anxiety. Our economic crisis has witnessed, at least some people, seeing things prior to it as 'being mad', 'getting out of hand', 'being run off my feet'. There is some sense in which the current situation may be a respite, and perhaps even an opportunity. Yet for others, it is a dire and dark place, putting intolerable pressures on families and communities; driving some to leave the country and others to leave this life. Our focus in this book is not just for the wildly optimistic. We don't underestimate the real misery some people are experiencing, but we do believe that a country more orientated towards achieving happiness can be of real benefit to all. In this book we present simple suggestions for improving happiness, both at the national and at an individual level. We believe that government, organisations and individuals now need to orientate their manifestos, targets and motivations to promote the happiness and well-being of our greatest natural resource – our people.

We would like to thank a number of supporters and funders of the National Happiness Experiment. Dublin City of Science 2012 and Vodafone have been major stalwarts, as have the Science Gallery, the School of Psychology and the Centre for Global Health in Trinity. In Chapter 2, where we describe the procedure of the National Happiness Experiment, we say our thanks in a bit more detail and so won't labour it here.

We have included the questions of the National Happiness Experiment in an appendix so anyone who missed out can score themselves and compare it to the national results.

We hope in reading this book, not only might it make you more aware of the things that might make you happier personally, but also more interested in what should be done to make everyone else happier too.

Chapter One

WHO WANTS TO BE HAPPY?

WHAT IS HAPPINESS?

This, as you can imagine, is not an easy question to answer because individuals differ in interests, preferences, values and so on. At a very general level happiness can be understood to have three basic components.[2] One of these, and perhaps how many people intuitively think of happiness, is having positive emotions, about the past, present and future. In terms of the past people may look back with contentment, or forgiveness; in the present they may feel joy; and they may have great optimism about the future. This component is therefore basically about having a *pleasant life*. A second component is about having a *meaningful life*; where people feel a strong attachment to something greater than themselves, which gives a sense of purpose. This could be God, country, sport, community, or a whole range of ideas that people choose to identify

5

themselves with, and in doing so become 'more than' just themselves. The third component is about having an *engaged life*; feeling totally absorbed in some activity or belief, anything from stamp collecting to surfing, where people feel totally 'in the zone'; when you are doing that activity you are totally focused and time can easily pass you by without a notice.

Already, you may be thinking that some of these ideas are not so much about 'happiness' and more about 'satisfaction'. In fact, each of these three components – pleasure, meaning and engagement – have been shown to make significant and independent contributions to life satisfaction, but meaning and engagement make the greatest contribution to life satisfaction.[3] So nobody would deny the important role pleasure has in our lives, but the exclusive focus on pleasure has sometimes backfired on people as we embark on a 'hedonic treadmill' chasing the next treat, the next gadget, the next 'fix', as our level of happiness stays still, or even declines.[4] In this book we are going to be exploring life satisfaction along with happiness, accepting that they may be over-lapping and related but are not necessarily the same.

As will be seen one of the factors associated with happiness is in fact tolerance, and so it is important not to be too dogmatic about exactly what constitutes happiness and in what proportion. While we will demonstrate the recipe for happiness has certain key ingredients, individuals may want a bit more of this, or a bit less of that, to float their boat. It would be very boring if the same quantities of everything produced the same effects on everyone. Indeed, there would be no need for psychologists!

Different ways of measuring happiness emphasise different combinations of these three ways of living happiness and so we will report on a number of different aspects of happiness. However, probably the most widely used measure of happiness doesn't ask people what makes them happy, but rather just how happy they feel – regardless of the reason. This measure, first used by Hadley Cantril in 1965,[5] simply asked people to indicate which step they felt they stood on given an imaginary ladder where the first (bottom) step (step 0) represented the worst possible life for them, and the top step (step 10) represented the best possible life. This measure has subsequently been used in many studies and has provided some interesting and surprising insights into happiness. Below we review some of the 'stand out' results from happiness research, using both the Cantril ladder measurement technique as well as other related measures of happiness and life satisfaction.

INCOME

It may be no surprise that on average richer people are happier than poorer people; after all, the richer you are then the better chance you have of getting high quality education, better nutrition, better healthcare and so on. What is more surprising is research indicating that as the average income in a population increases, its members don't necessarily get any happier. For instance, although incomes in Germany rose steadily over the past 40 years, life satisfaction hasn't; it has shown similar results across this time span, indicating that it has remained virtually static. In the USA, where average incomes have also increased over recent decades, there is actually a downward trend for happiness over the last 30 years – so, if anything, people are less happy now than they were when they were poorer.[6] How can this be?

It seems that – at least in relatively wealthy countries like Ireland – it is the relative distribution of income, or how much one person gets in comparison to another, rather than the absolute level of income, that is most closely associated with life satisfaction. So while someone may be earning a good income, if they feel that they are earning too little compared with others, or indeed that they are earning too much relative to others, they may be less satisfied.[7] This is just one example of a broad range of research which effectively demonstrates that people feel better when they are living in a society where there is a sense that resources and rewards are distributed fairly. This idea of social justice is much broader than income[8] and can relate to many different aspects of work life, such as recognition, promotion, the application of fair procedures, including wrong-doers getting their appropriate punishment.[9] So, in terms of income the simple message is that increasing average incomes won't make us happier; rather, it's how we distribute income as well as other indications that we live in a fair society.

INEQUALITY

It's worth thinking about – from a psychological and social point of view – why inequality is such a problem. One suggestion is that it increases social tension between the 'haves' and the 'have nots', and it seems that the existence of such tension can reduce happiness, not just for the poor but for the rich as well.[6] In fact, the effects of inequality reach much further than you might think. In societies – especially rich societies, like ours – where there is greater inequality, its members have poorer health. This is the case for both mental health problems like depression and physical health problems like cardiovascular disease. In societies where the provision of healthcare is itself very unequal – where for instance the rich have better access to healthcare than the poor – we might, ironically, expect the inequality in the health system itself to be one of the key factors contributing to people's lower life satisfaction and greater health problems.

There is another, economic, argument for addressing inequality. This is referred to as the marginal utility of income. For example, the benefit of say an extra €100 in someone's pocket will depend on their normal earnings. Someone who earns €1,000 a month is going to be able to get more benefit from an extra €100 than someone who earns €10,000 a month, or someone who earns €100,000 a month. The extra demand and consumption of services and goods will be felt to be more beneficial by people with less money.

As we will see shortly, there is now convincing evidence that countries with higher levels of income inequality suffer from greater unhappiness, but also from a whole range of mental and physical health problems, and this relationship seems to be causal.[10] So how government distributes income, how wide is the gap between the best off and the worst off, what gets prioritised in the good times and what gets cut in the bad times – all of these decisions can be expected to affect happiness and well-being.

EMPLOYMENT

One of the most devastating effects of the recession has surely been the loss of jobs and the associated emigration of people who would otherwise have wished to stay in Ireland. Apart from those leaving for distant places – a haemorrhaging of talents to Australia, USA, Canada – there is also the seeping wounds of families where one partner has to work abroad returning at weekends, as time and money allow. For job-seekers, not having a job is terrible. It's terrible because of a loss of income, but it's also terrible because jobs can contribute to giving people a sense of meaning and purpose. It allows individuals to feel that they are making a useful contribution to a community, which also contributes to their own self-esteem and happiness. While it may be that 'quality' jobs are most sought after, the research evidence suggests that for most individuals, regardless of their background, any job is better than none at all.[11] It also seems that part-time jobs can bolster an individual's sense of self-worth, as well as sharing the financial benefits of work over a greater range of people. So job-sharing (working only part-time), a common practice in Germany, seems to be better at retaining 'social capital' than having some people full-time employed and others unemployed. A job gives a person a sense of being a member of a community and an opportunity to interact with others.

The above facets of a job of course contribute to 'social capital': a very nice term because it reminds us that how we feel about ourselves and others in a society has real value, but also, like financial capital, it can be frittered away, squandered, so that people feel that others around them are no good, not worthy and so on. How do we feel about other's willingness to help us and how might this be related to happiness and satisfaction?

TRUST

That idea of social capital is also linked to the idea of having trust in others. What is your 'radius of trust'? Do you trust family members, neighbours, strangers? Do you trust people you work with (if you have a job)? The Lost Wallet Experiment is a lovely methodology for estimating the extent of trust in others. Wallets with cash in them, along with a name and address of the supposed owner, are dropped in the street and the number returned is seen as one index of trust. When this is done across different countries, then it can provide some indication of comparative trust, and in fact has been found to correlate well with other measures of trust.[12] So, if you going to drop your wallet or purse, where is the best place to do it, in terms of the likelihood of getting it back? Answer? To our knowledge this hasn't been tried in Ireland. What do you think are the chances of getting your wallet back if you dropped it in your local high street? One of us recently left an iPhone in a toilet in Cape Town, to find it had been handed in by the toilet cleaner. The iPhone probably cost more than the cleaner's monthly wage. That may not be your media image of South Africa, but it goes to show that good people are all around us, and it is hugely affirming of oneself and humanity when people can be trusted.

The evidence suggests that trust causes happiness rather than the other way around. Of course, the reverse may also apply. Working with people you can't trust evaporates social capital. Ireland has had to shoulder a litany of untrustworthy characters in the public eye in recent years, ranging from corrupt politicians to abusive clergy to greedy developers and bankers – in a sense, all have broken the 'bond of trust' that exists between the population at large and the people who occupy positions of authority.

This also relates to what is known as the 'psychological contract'. A legal contract between two parties stipulates in exact written terms what the obligations and rights of each party are. A psychological contract is not written down, it's implicit and often vague, but it's basically about what each party expects from the other, how they expect them to behave. There can be a psychological contract between different sectors of society and society as a whole. Society may, for instance, expect doctors to be more interested in health than money; and may become disillusioned with them working in lucrative private practice whilst drawing huge public sector salaries. Society may become disillusioned with judges who expound justice, but feel that they should not be subject to the same salary cuts as other civil servants. Society may become disillusioned by professors who are against the rich paying third level fees while the universities are left without the income to pay their own high salaries. All of these may be seen to be breaches of the psychological contract which professions have with society. The maintenance and enhancement of social capital is a challenge for all of us, not just the developers and bankers. Perhaps one of the most interesting questions we could ask is if people feel that powerful people who have done wrong are held to account in Ireland, and how do views about that relate to happiness?

The idea of social capital can be subdivided into what is called 'bonding capital' and 'bridging capital'. Bonding capital relates to strengthening relations between people who are seen as similar to each other, while bridging capital refers to strengthening relations between people who are seen as different from each other. Feeling good about those who are like you needs to be complimented by feeling good about those who are different. Vive la différence! Improved racial tolerance has been associated with increased happiness.[13] Bonding and bridging capital may be related to the sense of pride that people have in their identity. If we were to ask people how proud they are to be Irish (perhaps closer to bonding capital), or European (perhaps closer to bridging capital), what would they say, and how would these be related to happiness and satisfaction?

RELIGION

Does religion make you happy? Some may well argue that the function of religion is not necessarily to make you happy in the moment, but to give you a connection with a higher purpose. Research suggests that there is no difference in scores of life satisfaction (perhaps a better measure than happiness in this context) between more and less religious countries. However, it's more complicated than that. For instance, where life is hard (lower life expectancy, poorer education, less 'development'), those countries that are more religious have more people expressing positive emotions and fewer people expressing negative emotions. Where life is easier religion seems to make no difference to life satisfaction, for a country's population overall[14] – more religious countries are on average not happier or more satisfied than less religious countries. However, if one just looks at the individual level, there appears to be a small association such that those who are more religious are less likely to report depressive symptoms. Finally, of two key aspects of religious experience – the personal, such as prayer, and the social, such as support from others – each seems to be equally important for people who benefit from religion. Given the religious flux that Ireland has experienced over the past decade, it will be very interesting to see just what is the relationship between religion and happiness and satisfaction.

ALTRUISM

It is reassuring to know that people who care more about others are happier than those who care less. In one lovely experiment one group of people were given money to spend on shopping for others, while another group were given the same amount of money to spend on shopping for themselves. At the end of the shopping trip those who had spent the money on others were happier.[15] In fact, it seems that the giving of money to good causes is associated with activation of reward areas in the brain[16] – people like giving. The good news is that this sort of altruism isn't an innate ability or predisposition, it is something that can actually be developed in others. Following a two-week training course on compassion, those who did the course gave more money to a good cause in a laboratory game, relative to a comparison group who didn't complete the training, and at the same time showed more neural activity in the reward centres in their brains.[17] Given Ireland's history of giving at home and abroad, is our giving related to our happiness and satisfaction? How might our recession affect our feelings of altruism, and our belief in other people?

HEALTH

We have already alluded to the relationship between economic crisis and personal, family and community despair. It seems intuitively obvious that happiness and good mental health go together, and thus diminishing happiness is associated with poorer mental health. Depression, 'the common cold of psychopathology', is now recognised as one of the most disabling health conditions, often impairing people's thinking, limiting their activity and diminishing their participation in society.

Happiness also affects physical health. For instance, happier people tend to have better functioning immune systems, which means that if two people are exposed to the common cold virus, the happier one is more likely to successfully fight off the virus and therefore less likely to actually 'get' a cold, to develop symptoms.[18] Indeed, negative mood states are associated with premature death and increased risk of coronary heart disease as well as type 2 diabetes.[19] However, positive mood states are associated with reduced neuroendocrine, inflammatory, and cardiovascular activity – which is good! These effects are independent of age, gender, socioeconomic position, body mass or even smoking. The same researchers found that happier people had a more moderate biological response when they participated in mental stress testing. So happiness has a very positive health dividend, and of course healthy people put fewer demands on already overburdened health services.

Given our aging population in Ireland we are expecting greater health service demands from this group. What if their happiness could be a buffer? In a sample of adults spanning early to very late adulthood, followed up over 10 years, aging was found to be associated with more positive overall emotional well-being and with greater emotional stability[20] – in fact, this is a well-known effect. Dramatically, those individuals who experienced relatively more positive than negative emotions in everyday life were more likely to have survived 13 years later, and this held true when differences in age, sex, and ethnicity were taken into account. In this context, then, it will be interesting to see how happiness across the nation varies with age.

CONCLUSION

Who wants to be happy? It's pretty obvious that we all do, but what is less obvious perhaps are the benefits of happiness not just for the individuals themselves, but also for the community, indeed the nation. It makes good sense for 'us' to want as many people as possible to be happy, because it will improve the quality of life, indeed the length of life, for many. There are clear policy choices that can be made that are likely to increase happiness.

In this brief chapter we have summarised only some of the research on happiness, some of its determinants and some of its benefits. To quite an impressive extent, we actually do know how to make people happier! In the next chapter we describe the National Happiness

Experiment, which was an attempt to take the mood and satisfaction pulse of the nation over a six-week period in 2012, and to explore the relationship between feelings of happiness and life satisfaction and some of the other factors that we have described above. While we expected many of the results from above to hold up in Ireland, we are also aware that our own cultural[21] and socioeconomic conditions might affect these relationships in important ways. Let's see if they do.

Chapter 2

THE NATIONAL HAPPINESS
EXPERIMENT

In this chapter we briefly describe how we actually went about doing the National Happiness Experiment (NHE). The NHE was coordinated by ourselves, supported by Dublin City of Science and Vodafone, as well as by the Science Gallery, the School of Psychology and the Centre for Global Health in Trinity College Dublin, and implemented by Phonovation. This range of scientific, communications and commercial expertise allowed us to develop a unique 'experiment' where participants were recruited by free texting a number to Phonovation, signing up for the NHE, which allowed participants to receive and free-text respond to questions about happiness and satisfaction on a weekly basis, over a six-week period. In addition, each week we also asked questions that might have an influence on happiness and satisfaction.

It is important to point out that the NHE was not an 'experiment' in the sense that we were manipulating or trying to trick people. Rather, it was an experiment in the sense that we were seeing how events over six weeks might influence people – if, for instance, those who voted in the EU referendum were happier than those who didn't vote? Did the weather over the six weeks influence people's happiness? Did being happy one week predict being happy in future weeks? However, as indicated in Chapter 1, we were also interested to find out how other factors, like age, health, having children, being married, being religious, being always contactable, experiencing and doing good deeds and so on might influence happiness and satisfaction, and so we also asked specific questions each week, changing the topic of these questions, week by week.

We believe the NHE is unique and are not aware of any other research of this type conducted on a weekly basis over six weeks. In particular, we wanted to interrupt people's daily lives as they happened, asking pertinent questions; we didn't want to bring them into the more artificial (but more controlled) setting of a 'laboratory'. In a sense, for six weeks, our laboratory was Ireland! Thus the NHE came after and complimented the HAPPY? Exhibition, run by the School of Psychology in the Science Gallery, where people came into Trinity to do computer-based experiments. That exhibition, overseen by our colleague Ian Robertson, produced useful data, but in the NHE we wanted to take the 'lab' to the people, keenly aware that not everyone is able to, or wants to, come into a university to 'do experiments'.

We are tremendously grateful to the people who participated in the NHE, some of whom had also come to the HAPPY? Exhibition, but many of whom 'joined up' as a result of hearing about it on the national media. We owe a special vote of thanks to a range of media whose coverage of HAPPY? and/or the NHE helped us to recruit participants for the latter. For print media this included *Totally Dublin*, *The Irish Times*, *The Irish Independent*, *The Irish Examiner*, *The Evening Herald*, *The Sunday Independent*, *The Metro Herald*, *The Irish Star* and the *Irish Sun*. Internationally, *New Scientist* (online) and *The Lancet* noted it. Broadcast media included *The John Murray Show* on RTÉ Radio 1, *Drive* on BBC News Radio, *Moncrieff* on Newstalk, *Futureproof* on Newstalk, Highland radio and SPIN. Vodafone messaging its 'top-up' customers gave us a direct link into phone users; Vodafone also sponsored participation regardless of service provider. To all of these groups, and especially the Science Gallery, who so professionally facilitated these links, a huge 'thank ye!' for putting the research into the nation's consciousness.

In all, 3,309 people participated, three-quarters of whom were female – an interesting finding in itself. The participation level remained extremely high over the six-week period – with around 80 per cent of people staying the distance, an exceptionally high level of participation for this type of research. A 'back of the envelope' estimate would allow you to work out that with over 3,300 people, multiplied by an average of nine questions a week, over six weeks, this gave use approximately 180,000 data points – a small number in terms of Irish bank debt, but a good-sized one from which to draw some conclusions about happiness! We are also very grateful to David Hevey for his statistical expertise in helping us to analyse these results.

Happiness is complex and can be linked to individual factors like genetics, personality and behaviour, as well as social, societal and environmental factors. Below we have set out a simple model to highlight some of the key determinants of happiness and how they might combine to result in our individual and collective happiness (see Model A below). We then designed our experiment to investigate some elements of each of these dimensions to see how any or all of the areas we probed might contribute to Irish people's happiness levels (see Model B below).

Model A – The Web of Happiness

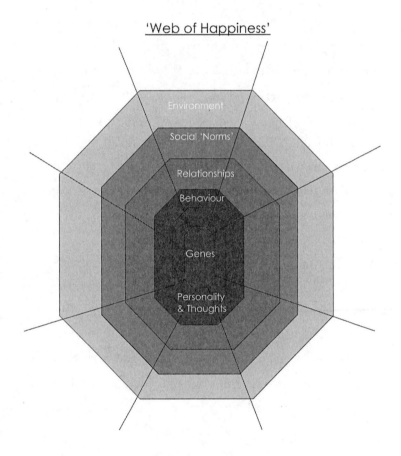

'Web of Happiness'

Environment

Social 'Norms'

Relationships

Behaviour

Genes

Personality & Thoughts

We now present the 'top cut' of the results. Our description of them here will not be comprehensive or too in depth; rather, we extract findings that we hope will be of greatest interest and will try to present them in a form that we hope most people will find accessible.

Further and much more academic-type publications will undertake more complex analysis, the re-

Model B – National Happiness Experiment Design

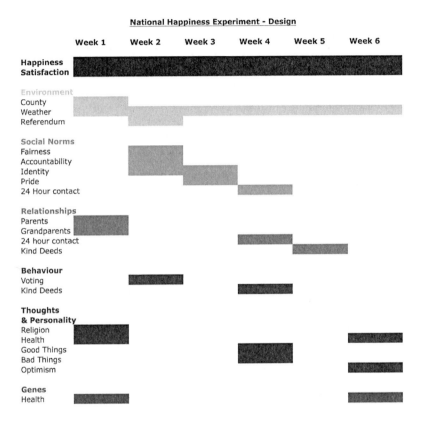

National Happiness Experiment - Design

	Week 1	Week 2	Week 3	Week 4	Week 5	Week 6

porting of which will doubtless be somewhat more impenetrable! Just a word of caution first: while some of the results can be observed over several weeks, many of our questions ask about a certain attribute just once and we explore its relationship with happiness and satisfaction.

As such, for some of our findings we cannot infer causality – we can't say that one thing actually causes another thing – but we can note association, where one thing happening tends to be associated with another thing happening. So, if on some occasions our conclusions are rather more tentative than you would wish, then this may be the reason why.

Chapter 3

RESULTS FROM THE NATIONAL HAPPINESS EXPERIMENT

I n this chapter we report on some of the results of the National Happiness Experiment. Where helpful we also try to consider previous research that allows us to place the Irish experience in a broader global context regarding happiness, satisfaction and related concepts.

THE ALL-IRELAND HAPPINESS CUP?

Are people in some counties happier than those in others? Figures 1 and 2 indicate responses from those who participated and who texted us the car registration letters (e.g. KE, WX, MO) of the county they lived in. We averaged these responses over the six weeks as the figures were quite stable over that period.

Figure 1: Happiness by County Averaged Over Six Weeks

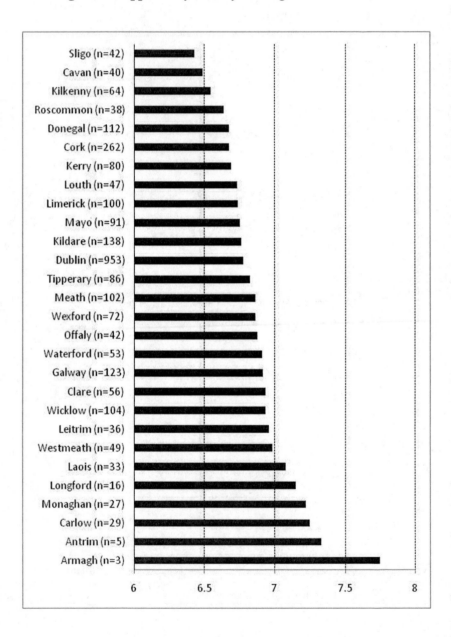

Figure 2: Satisfaction by County Averaged Over Six Weeks

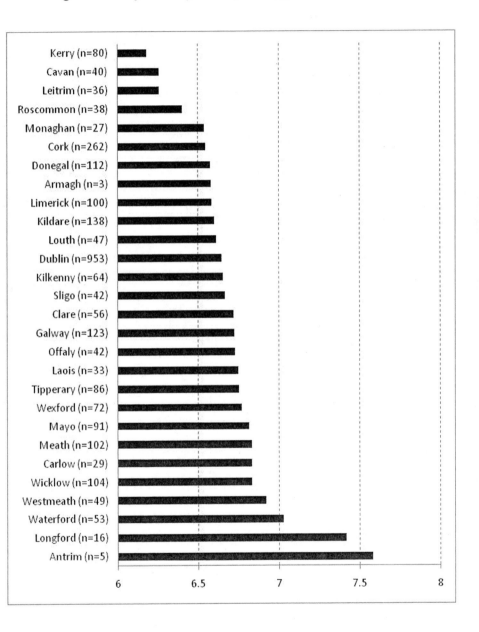

While it appears that there are indeed differences in happiness and satisfaction between counties, in fact, these differences are so small (we have 'stretched' just a small section of the horizontal axes on the bottom to emphasise the differences) that the good news is: we are all just about as happy and satisfied as each other regardless of which county we live. The county next door is not 'greener' and they are not having a better time over there!

Something else is striking: there are very different numbers of people responding from different counties – from three people in Armagh to 953 in Dublin. However, looking at the counties that did have a reasonable number of respondents, we can say that there are a fair number of people in Sligo who are less happy than the national average, and a fair number in Kerry who are less satisfied than the national average. Similarly, Carlow has a reasonable number of people scoring above the average happiness score and Waterford likewise for satisfaction.

While these differences between counties are interesting, it's important to repeat that they are not statistically significant, which means that these differences occur randomly, by chance, rather than having a meaningful pattern to them. We had wondered if the ratings in different counties could be influenced by variations in other factors – age, religion or health perhaps? While we certainly have interesting results in terms of these factors to describe below, none of them significantly affected the scores of happiness and satisfaction across the counties.

Our responses came from 28 of the 32 counties on the island and so are pretty comprehensive, but of course the numbers responding in each county differ quite dramatically. It is important to reiterate that to illustrate the pattern as clearly as possible we have focused on just the small range on the horizontal axis that people used – so in actual fact, all counties scored on average a score of 6 or above on the 1-10 rating scale for both happiness and satisfaction – no one county was miserable and no one county was ecstatic either. The All-Ireland Happiness Cup seems to be a comprehensive draw – all must have prizes!

An obvious question is, 'Why are ratings of happiness and satisfaction not the same'? Across the six weeks ratings of each were very strongly correlated, and it was possible to predict one week's ratings by looking at the previous week's rating of either happiness or satisfaction. However, it is also clear that they don't measure the same thing, and the extent to which they differ also varies by county (recall our discussion of happiness and satisfaction in Chapter 1). On average our ratings on the 10 point scale (1-10) were slightly higher for happiness than they were for life satisfaction, but there was very little difference. In Appendix 1 we compare Irish ratings on happiness and satisfaction with those world-wide, and it is clear that Ireland generally rates very well on these, usually in the top ten countries, depending on how the question is asked.

Nonetheless, we can see from our data that happiness and satisfaction do not always go together; they are measuring different things.[22] While there was a close relationship between them on a weekly basis, even the strongest weekly correlation (r = .74) could only explain about 50 per cent of the variance between the two scores – in other words, if you used the score on one (say, happiness) to predict the score on the other (say, life satisfaction), you would only be correct about half of the time. It may be that happiness is more directly mood-related and satisfaction is more of a reflective judgement, where people weigh up more aspects of their life experience, and this 'weighing' can be influenced by various factors, including cognitive biases (see also Chapter 1). By following the results below, you will get some insight into which factors weigh more in terms of influencing people's estimates of their happiness and satisfaction.

FAMILY AND AGE

The average age of our participants was 44 years, ranging from under 10 (one actually claiming to be a very precocious two!) up to 84. Figure 3 plots happiness by age and Figure 4 plots satisfaction by age.

Figure 3: Happiness by Age as a Scatter Plot

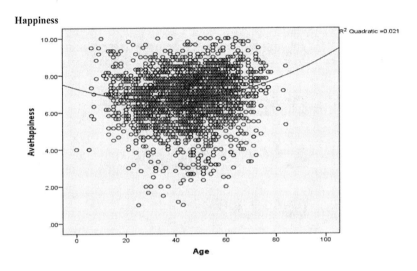

Figure 4: Satisfaction by Age as a Scatter plot

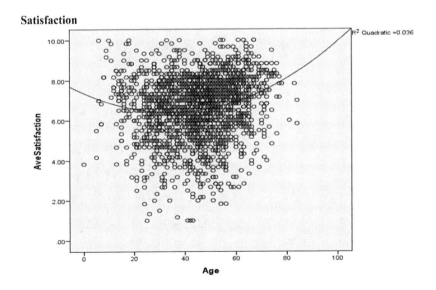

Figure 5: Happiness by Age Range as a Bar Graph

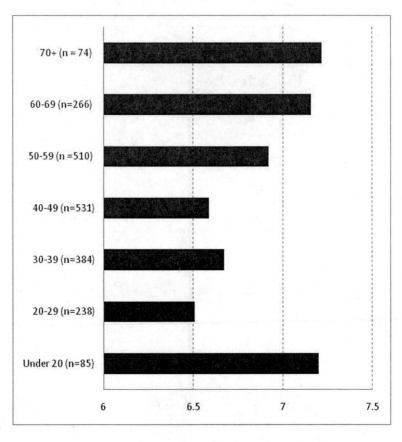

The results are really very interesting. By using complex statistical analysis and imposing a 'line of best fit' for the data, it can be seen that for both happiness and satisfaction the younger and older age groups (those up to 20 and 60+) are the happiest and most satisfied, while those in the 'middle years' are struggling more. What is really nice to know is that the best times are ahead! Both of these quadratic relationships – as

Figure 6: Satisfaction by Age Range as a Bar Graph

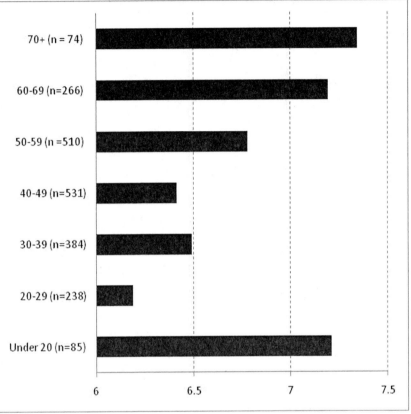

they are called – are statistically significant. A slightly different way of summarising the data is shown in Figures 5 and 6, and this makes it easier to see how those in their 20s, 30s and 40s are less happy and satisfied than the rest of us. For instance, those in their 20s are significantly less happy and significantly less satisfied than those under 20, and those in their 50s, 60s and 70s. While similar relationships between age and happiness and satisfaction are also found in other countries,[23] it is important that we appreciate the burden that our 'twenty/thirty/forty-somethings' carry, and that we address this in Ireland.

We reported above that happiness and satisfaction do not vary dramatically by county, but Figures 3 and 4 above – plotting individual's responses – do illustrate they vary quite dramatically between individuals. Each circle represents one or more individual's response, more if numerous people of that age gave the same response. Despite our currently difficult circumstances, there are individuals who are really very happy and satisfied, scoring at the top of the scale; but there are also individuals who are really struggling, scoring at the bottom of the scale. We will discuss this in the next chapter.

It is widely believed that children are one of the joys of life and contribute much to an individual's happiness. On first look, our results supported this, however a closer examination shows it's more complicated than that. People are either parents, or not parents, and if they are parents, they may also be grandparents. If we compare the happiness scores of those who are parents or grandparents with those who don't have children, then we find that the parents or grandparents are happier than those who are not parents. However, once you take into account that, on average, parents and grandparents are older, then the effect disappears

– having children appears to have no beneficial effect, in terms of happiness.

Interestingly, the story is a bit different for ratings of satisfaction. Those who are both parents and grandparents rated themselves as being significantly more satisfied with life, than those who were either just parents, or those without children, and this effect was stable across the five weeks that we measured it. These results are going to be analysed in much more depth by other colleagues in the School of Psychology at Trinity College. But in summary, from this very brief look, it seems that having children doesn't necessarily boost your happiness but they do make their grandparents feel more satisfied – maybe there is a baby-sitting angle to be worked on there?!

In fact, the finding that having children in itself doesn't make you happier doesn't just apply to Ireland, but elsewhere as well. However, it seems that the time when children make you most happy is when they are between the ages of 3-12,[6] that is, when they are able to understand what you want them to do, and less able to refuse to do it!

There was no difference in the happiness or satisfaction of men and women, although in many high-income countries, women are found to be more satisfied with life.[6] We didn't ask our participants if they were married or had a partner so the happiness of Irish partnerships remains a mystery! Other research suggests that marriage is good for you, in the sense that it increases life satisfaction.[6] Aside from love and companionship marriage can also, of course, offer an economic buffer allowing people to have better physical and psychological health and to live longer.[6]

RELIGION

Ireland has had a complex history with religion, its divisions ravaging our island, its teachings dogmatic and its practice ranging from global missionary and the backbone of community cohesion to heinous child abuse and the taking of children from young mothers. We were therefore keen to see how religion related to happiness and satisfaction in 2012. Our results show that the more religious people are, on average, the happier they are, and the more satisfied with life. Having said that, although these effects are statistically significant, they are really rather small effects ($r = 0.12$ and $r = 0.13$ respectively), indicating that they have a statistically significant but actually quite small influence on happiness and satisfaction, but are nonetheless noteworthy.

Religion is one of the variables on which there were differences between a few counties. Recall that people were rating how religious they felt they were (not how often they attended religious services) on a scale form 1-10, where 1 represented 'Not at All' and 10 represented 'Very Much'. The highest self-rated religious counties were Armagh (with an average rating

Figure 7: Religiosity Rating by County

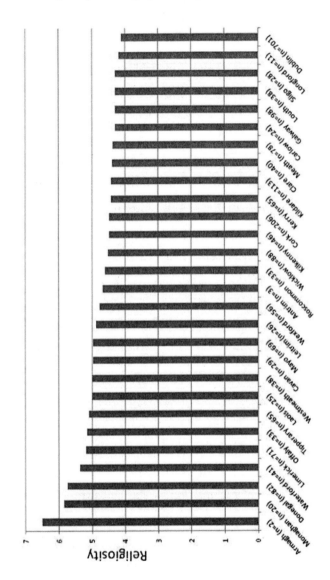

of 6.5), Monaghan (5.8) and Donegal (5.7), while the least religious was Dublin (average rating 4.1). The difference between these three and Dublin were statistically significant. Importantly, we were able to rerun our analysis to see if these differences in religiosity were a product of the age of the respondents differing across counties, and found that these differences in religiosity persisted when we controlled for age. So, it wasn't just the 'young yuppies' in Dublin and 'The Pale' that accounted for the results, it applied across the age range. However, even the people from the county that had the highest self-rated religiosity scored just 6.5 on a ten point scale, with others scoring around 4. With an average overall score of just 4.5 on a 10 point scale this suggests that a fair proportion of the population doesn't see religion as a major part of their life. This has important implications for the role of religion in our schools, which we will discuss in the next chapter.

Finally, just to put this in a broader perspective, as we stated in Chapter 1, in well-off countries generally there is no relationship between religiosity and happiness or satisfaction, while in poorer countries more religious people tend to have more a 'positive affect' (that is, feel good more of the time). The Irish results are therefore of particular interest because we seem to be 'bucking the trend' – perhaps despite relative wealth in global terms, the current climate of 'austerity' means that people are finding religion a useful 'buffer' against despair?

HEALTH

In Chapter 1 we highlighted the strong relationship between health, happiness and satisfaction – indeed, that phrase just seems to roll off the tongue. Well it might: there was a very strong positive correlation between health and happiness ($r = 0.46$) and an even stronger one between health and satisfaction ($r = 0.50$), and so proud of it are we, that we have plotted it below in Figure 8. This has important social implications, which we will return to in the next chapter.

THE WEATHER

That topic of endless conversations, on which we are all such great experts (or used to be when 'weather was weather') has surprisingly little effect on our happiness or satisfaction. Perhaps just as well. During the NHE the weather was 'poor'; there was plenty of it, but just the wrong type. We tracked weather by Met Éireann reports and matched these to the regions that people were texting us from; thus we were able to take into account weather variation across the country on the same day. During the days of our weekly texting we had 'rainy', 'cloudy' and 'partly cloudy' most of the time, and very little 'sunny'. Across these categories of weather

Figure 8: Relationship between Satisfaction and Health

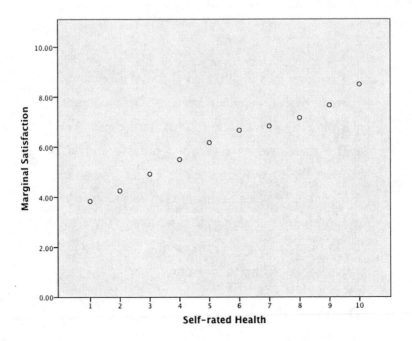

there was no relationship between them and happiness or satisfaction. We also examined temperature variation, but again there was no relationship. Perhaps given the very poor summer it could be argued that we didn't have enough good weather to really compare effectively with the poor weather – so let's not give up on the value of elusive sunny days just yet.

VOTING AND IDENTITY

The period of our study coincided with the Referendum on 2012 European Fiscal Compact, a.k.a. the Treaty of Stability. While we felt that asking people how they had voted – our texting took place on the day after the vote – might be too intrusive, we wanted to know simply whether people did, or didn't, vote. Was participating in the vote – participative democracy – related to happiness or satisfaction? No. Of those in the sample who responded to this question, those who said they voted (72 per cent) were not significantly happier or more satisfied that week, the following week or on average, than those who said they didn't vote (28 per cent). Of course, it may be that Referenda on European issues may not be as critical to the identity of Irish people as are issues more confined to the island itself, or it may be that the subject matter of the referendum was inherently 'depressing' and counteracted any positive lift from partaking in the vote.

We also asked people about how proud they were to be 1) Irish and 2) European, and looked at the relationship between these feelings of pride and happiness and satisfaction, both at the time of the question and the average score across the NHE. There was a significant correlation between having a sense of pride and happiness that day and on average for both 'Irishness' and 'Europeanness'; in fact, the effects were equally strong. Surprising to us was that the strongest of all these effects was the relationship between feeling pride in being European and a high level of average satisfaction across the weeks (r = .32).

ORGANISATIONAL JUSTICE AND ACCOUNTABILITY

At least one of the prevalent narratives for explaining the economic (and of course social and psychological) crisis in Ireland has been that powerful people did not exercise due diligence, either in the regulation or conduct of business; that we are now all paying for their mistakes; and that they themselves have not been held accountable for their actions. If this is indeed the case, how might these feelings of injustice influence happiness and satisfaction? We asked participants if they felt that powerful people in Ireland were held to account for their misdoings.

TABLE 1: MEAN ANSWERS TO QUESTIONS ON FAIRNESS, ACCOUNTABILITY AND IDENTITY

Questions Asked	*Mean Score* *1 (low)–10 (high)*
In general, do you feel that Ireland is a fair place?	*5.14*
In general, do you feel that powerful people are kept in check by media, law and public opinion?	*3.79*
In general, do you feel that Ireland has a unique and valuable identity?	*7.53*

It's clear that the majority of respondents feel that Ireland has a unique and valuable identity – we still feel that there is something good about Ireland! However, with a score of only just over 5 out of 10, we seem to be quite ambivalent – as a group – about whether it's a fair place to live – a lot of us think not. Furthermore, a low score, below 4, indicates that most of us don't think it's a country where powerful people are kept in check. For all of these questions, significant correlations showed that people who scored higher on them were also more likely to rate themselves as being happier. The relationship between each of them and satisfaction was stronger still. This demonstrates very clearly that a sense of fairness, accountability and identity are significantly associated with happiness and life satisfaction for people in Ireland; and so to the extent that we lack these, they may well diminish our happiness and life satisfaction.

Interestingly, these results were the same for men and women. Across the age range scores did vary however. There was a small tendency for older people to more strongly feel that Ireland had a unique and valuable identity. However, quadratic equations showed a U-shaped relationship where those in the 30s-50s age range gave the lowest ratings for fairness and accountability. We will have a good deal more to say about these findings and their implications for Irish institutions – such as health and education – in Chapter 4.

24-HOUR LIFE

We asked people if they felt that it was good being contactable by others up to 24 hours a day through use of their mobile phone ('These days you can be contacted most times of the day and night – on a scale of 1 to 10 how happy does this make you feel?'). Remember, respondents were all phone users as these questions were asked through texting. We also asked them if they felt it was good that they could contact others 24 hours a day ('These days you can contact other people most times of the day and night – on a scale of 1 to 10 how happy does this make you feel?')

	Can Be Contacted by Others 24/7 Mean Happiness Score Out of 10
Under 20	*6.75*
20–29	*6.12*
30–39	*5.72*
40–49	*5.62*
50–59	*5.97*
60–69	*6.43*
70+	*6.93*

	Can Contact Others 24/7 Mean Happiness Score Out of 10
Under 20	*7.70*
20-29	*7.25*
30-39	*6.49*
40-49	*6.55*
50-59	*7.02*
60-69	*7.35*
70+	*7.70*

The under 20s and over 70s scored significantly happier on both the idea of being contactable and being able to contact others 24/7. Although, across the board – and quite understandably – people valued being able to contact others more than being contactable by others.

Importantly, affirmative answers to both questions were positively associated with happiness and life satisfaction, both on the day we asked and on average across the NHE. People who feel good about phone use – in both directions – are significantly happier and more satisfied. It is worth noting that there was not any difference between males and females regarding their attitudes towards being contactable or being able to contact others. Finally, it seems that those who were grandparents felt especially happy about being able to contact and be contactable by others. This suggests an important intergenerational benefit of phone use that may not be fully appreciated.

GOOD THINGS

On Week 4 of the NHE we asked people about the number of positive things that had happened to them in the past 24 hours, expecting to find that people who recalled more positive things would be happier. That was not the case; there was no association between the two. However, this was not so with negative things that happened in the last 24 hours. While the number of negative things people reported wasn't associated with ratings of happiness and satisfaction on the same day, interestingly, it was associated with ratings of average happiness and average satisfaction across the NHE. In other words, ratings concerning the frequency of negative events were related to happiness and satisfaction even before those events ever happened. Although this may seem bizarre, in fact, it is well known that people who are sadder (less happy and satisfied) tend to recall more negative events happening to them than do people who are happier.[24] Thus, in our sample it may be that relatively sadder people simply recalled more negative events, rather than more negative events actually happening to them – a sort of glass half empty, rather than half full perspective. There was no difference in the number of positive or negative events recalled by males or females, nor was this related to age.

It is clear that people recalled more positive things happening to them – on average between four and five – in the last day, than negative things – close to two – in the last day. So there seems to be more than double the number of positive to negative events, but less than three times as many. Some researchers have suggested that one of the contributors to happiness is the ratio of positive to negative events, and that a ratio of 3:1 is a critical threshold.[25] We tested this out. There was no relationship between the size of this ratio and whether people felt happier, or more satisfied, either on the week we asked the question or on the subsequent week. This calls into question the idea of a 'magic ratio' between good and bad events being related to happiness.

How many positive things have happened to you in the last 24 hours?	*4.41*
How many negative things have happened to you in the last 24 hours?	*1.83*

We also asked people whether they had done good deeds for others in the last week or if other people had done good deeds for them. Here there was a ratio of about two good deeds done to every one received.

Have you done a kind deed for someone in the last week? If so, how many kind deeds?	2.41
Has anyone done a kind deed for you in the last week? If so, how many kind deeds?	1.69

We were surprised that there was no relationship between answers to the number of good deeds done or received and ratings of happiness or satisfaction on that day, or indeed on average Nor did the *ratio* of good deeds done/received have any association with happiness or satisfaction.

A week later we asked people to anticipate how likely it was that they would do a kind deed for others, and how likely they would be to ask for help from others. Interestingly, these questions produced a very different pattern of results. Firstly, people anticipated that they were very likely to do a kind deed (almost 8 out of 10) and reasonably likely (around 6 out of 10) to ask for help from others.

How likely would you be to do a kind deed for somebody in the next week?	7.70
How likely would you be to ask for help from others if you needed it, in the next week?	6.10

The answers to both of these questions were significantly and positively associated with happiness and satisfaction both that day and on average – those who were happier and more satisfied anticipated more kind deeds done by them and feeling more likely to ask for help, if needed. Perhaps this optimism – a sort of belief in the positive intention of others and of yourself – could be seen as an indication of the 'social capital' we mentioned in Chapter 1. We return to this in the next chapter.

OPTIMISM ABOUT THE FUTURE

More direct measures of optimism (but not necessarily social capital) were the two questions we asked about optimism for one's self and for Ireland. The answers to both of these questions were significantly associated with both happiness and satisfaction, on that day and on average.

How optimistic do you feel for your future?	*6.75*
How optimistic do you feel for Ireland's future?	*5.61*

The effects, both of which were quite strong, were however stronger for ratings of satisfaction than happiness, and for ratings of personal optimism than national optimism. Finally, ratings of both personal optimism and optimism about Ireland were both related to self-rated health ($r = 0.43$ and $r = 0.32$ respectively); thus personal optimism was the attitude most strongly related to health, and to happiness and satisfaction. This is consistent with other research that personal mindset is strongly linked to happiness levels.

THE EFFECTS OF FEEDBACK

Remember we said that the NHE wasn't an experiment in the sense that we manipulated people – well that's true, but we did vary one factor across people. To some people (chosen randomly by a computer programme) we sent feedback on some of the average (not individual) scores of the previous week. To others we didn't. In experimental terms this wasn't a 'pure' manipulation because all participants were made aware that summary results from previous weeks could be seen on the project website (which didn't always work, for which we do apologise). So, we don't know if some of the people who didn't get feedback sent to their phone actually went looking for the feedback on the website, or indeed if those who got feedback on their phone also checked out the website. What we do know is who was sent feedback on their phone and who wasn't. We were interested to see if getting feedback influenced people's willingness to participate in future weeks.

Yes it did. Feedback from Week 1 was sent in Week 2, and so in Week 3 we were able to see what effect it had. Of those who received feedback in Week 2, 95 per cent participated by sending responses in Week 3, while only 80 per cent of those who didn't get feedback in Week 2 responded in Week 3. However, even that 80 per cent is an incredibly high response rate for survey research of this kind. But it's clear that whether or not people got feedback did have a statistically significant influence on their decision to continue participating in the research.

These effects persisted in the subsequent weeks and by the last week, Week 6, 94 per cent of those who got feedback had continued, while 72 per cent of those who didn't get feedback had continued. We were delighted that so many people from both groups stuck with us through the six-week long period – thanks again! We will have more to say about the value of this sort of survey method, and of not 'keeping people in the dark', in the next chapter.

Chapter 4

What Can We Do?

So what would an Irish society – and an Irish economy – run 'as though people, and their happiness, mattered' – look like? As we showed earlier in our Web of Happiness, the happiness of individuals is built both from the 'inside-out' – from a combination of our genes, attitudes and behaviours – but also from the 'outside-in' – from environmental, societal and social factors. In this chapter we want to focus on just a few of the salient themes which we feel are of particular relevance to the Irish situation. The 'We' then is all of us collectively as Irish society, although politicians and policy makers clearly have a special role and responsibility here. The next chapter focuses on what 'You', as an individual, can do to affect your own happiness.

But before delving into policy issues, you might ask whether we should bother changing any policies when our happiness levels are relatively high in global terms?

'SURE AREN'T WE FAIRLY HAPPY ANYWAY ...'

It is true that Ireland comes out remarkably well when we are compared internationally on a broad range of measures of happiness, satisfaction, feelings about yesterday and so on. Perhaps we are simply 'happier', or more willing to present our happiness, or less willing to say we are unhappy. Perhaps also the people who decided to participate in the NHE were above average happiness compared to the rest of the country. Whatever is the case, the data we have both from the NHE and from other international surveys, censuses and polls make up the information available to us, which we need to try and make sense of. And so, it may be argued that as we are fairly happy as a country compared to other countries. Shouldn't we just 'get on with it', and wait for an upswing in the economy to make us all even happier?! Well, no. First of all, as shown in Chapter 1, there is now good evidence that increased income – and people having more 'stuff' – does not in itself result in greater happiness; indeed, happiness has 'flat-lined' (remained unchanged) in economies that have grown in strength over the last three to four decades, most notably, the USA and Germany.

Secondly, just because we come out well on measures of happiness or life satisfaction doesn't mean that everything is 'as good as it gets', or that the conditions that support our happiness couldn't be improved. For instance, even during what we euphemistically refer to as 'the Troubles', Irish levity and humour did not disappear, but no one would seriously suggest that means the people of Ireland were unaffected or didn't feel it was a priory for them to end the murder and mayhem wrecked on so many families. So, if indeed 'the Irish' are blessed with greater levity and enjoy more *craic* than many others, this should not be presented as a barrier towards making our society a better place to live.

Even more emphatically, while we – as psychologists – certainly do appreciate the importance of personal attitudes towards happiness (see Chapter 5 for more on this), and while there may be a place for the 'don't worry, be happy' philosophy, we can also do people a disservice by failing to recognise that many individuals are struggling, not necessarily because of their own shortcomings or their personal negativity but rather because they have been shunted into an economic, social and psychological 'siding' by an economy that has come off the rails. To build on this analogy, as we try to get our country back on track, we have an opportunity to consider where we should be going and who should be travelling with us. Below are a few travel companions who might make future travels not only 'happier', but also lead to the sort of place you might want to go.

The World Happiness Report warns that while increasing GDP (Gross Domestic Product) may be a valuable goal, it is certainly not the only goal nations should pursue, nor should it be pursued to the extent that 1) 'economic stability is imperilled'; 2) 'community cohesion is destroyed'; 3) 'the weak lose their dignity or place in the economy'; 4) 'ethical standards are sacrificed'; or 5) 'the environment, including climate, is put at risk'. Some may feel that all five of these 'damages' have been visited on Irish society in recent years. Certainly, our economic stability has self-evidently been shattered; our community cohesion – with ghost estates and sub-standard built homes – has been undermined; the most disadvantaged – such as people with disabilities or those caring for ill relatives at home – have been targeted for cuts in supports; some would feel that the ethics of paying back unsecured bond holders with money that could have addressed some of the above points is unethical; and our short-term desperation could mean we short-change our environmental safeguards. With all of these 'damages' done, it should renew our focus on solutions that can lead to better economic competitiveness, but not at the cost of our broader and longer-term human happiness and sustainability.

There are many possible policy implications that can be drawn from the NHE, and we do not attempt to address them all here. Instead, we will focus on some of the major policy issues facing Ireland, and how they may be informed by the results of the NHE, as well as related research. In particular, we consider the implications of our results on perceptions of how fair a country we consider Ireland to be, whether people are held accountable, people's sense of community and identity, the age at which people are happiest, optimism about the future, and the importance of keeping the populace motivated by keeping them informed.

EQUALITY AND INCLUSION

International research has clearly demonstrated that the more unequal a society is the more problems it has, regardless of its actual level of wealth.[26] In the NHE we found that, on average, people do not feel that Ireland is a particularly fair place, nor do they feel that powerful people are kept in check by media, law and public opinion. These 'discontents' are associated with less happiness and satisfaction. So what implications do these results about fairness have for two of our most important sectors in society – education and health?

We are known as 'Ireland of the welcomes' but do our systems for education and health represent an Ireland that welcomes everyone equally? Do we 'welcome' each other equally to participate in society and benefit from its opportunities?

EDUCATION

While it would be wonderful if the quality and standard of education were the same for all people everywhere, they are never likely to be. Even within one jurisdiction there will be regional variations and often significant differences within the same county, town or even community. In Ireland, one of the indices of educational success – going on to third level education – is strongly influenced not just by where your school is, but by whether it is a state school or a private one. While state education is provided for all, some choose to educate their children outside that system, and to send them to private schools where they may benefit from 'better' education, greater prestige, a more influential social network, or whatever. It is the right of any parent to choose what they see as an 'enhanced' education over what is offered by the state sector. Where this becomes difficult is the realisation that education is not just about achieving certain levels of learning or knowledge; it also about relative levels of learning or knowledge, that is, education is a competition. To get access to certain careers you need a certain number of points and, on average, it would seem that you're more likely to achieve those points in private than public schools. For many parents this argument is simply a 'no-brainer' – that's the very point of sending their kids to private school!

If this is an example of inequality what should the government's role be in it? Should the government provide financial support so that students going outside the state system have an advantage over those inside the state system? Surely not. Should the government spend more on the education of the wealthiest in society than it does on the poorest in society? Surely not. The government should allow for competition and choice, but not spend public money on promoting privilege. Surely, this too, is a 'no-brainer'.

A stronger sense of inclusion and togetherness is associated with greater well-being.[27] In Ireland, greater inclusion is a particular concern at primary level. *The Growing Up in Ireland* study found that the single biggest factor determining the performance of 9-year-old children across Ireland was the education level of their mothers: 36 per cent of children with graduate mothers were in the highest quintile for reading and maths, and only 11 per cent of children with mothers who left at lower secondary or before. The OECD 2011 study on *Overcoming School Failure* states that the number one priority is 'to make our education system better for disadvantaged children and families'. Various programmes ranging from the universal pre-school free year to tailored programmes for disadvantaged families have been rolled out and are being shown to make a positive difference.[28] Perhaps government should allocate more resources on supporting the primary and pre-primary levels of education; we know that the more privileged end of the spectrum is already overrepresented at third level.

HEALTH

Another sacred cow must surely be healthcare. Through the lens of equality the ability of half of the population to leap-frog the other half when they are ill – not on the basis of their health needs but on the basis of whether they can afford private healthcare – doesn't seem right; it's a sort of 'health apartheid'. Again, here the government is complicit in undermining its own system by supporting 'choice': the richer have more choice than the poorer; at least, that is the justification for private healthcare. In practice, this means that the richer can choose to get seen faster, and let's face it, if you have a serious health problem and have the money you would be mad not to avail of faster treatment, either for yourself or for your loved ones.

Healthcare staff send out confusing signals when employed by the state and at the same time being able to offer patients incentives to jump out of this system ('my waiting list is six months, but I could see you next week privately'), while still reaping the benefits of the system's staff, facilities and follow-up care. At the same time, some public patients end up waiting longer for the care they need, which as a result can end up costing the system more[29] because they are sicker by the time they receive treatment. Thus inequity 'costs' more, both in human and financial terms.

Our actual spend in 2012 on health in Ireland will be in line with the OECD average when we combine private and public spending.[30] This absolute level is unlikely to grow in the next few years of austerity. However, what can be changed is *how* we allocate our health spending and resources, and what we offer to whom, for what, and when. At best, a reform of the system should ensure that all people have access to basic health services. In addition, people could still take out private insurance to cover the 'hotel' aspects of healthcare (caviar for breakfast or brass knobs on the bed type of thing), but not access the public system for a consultation that facilitates private leap-frogging.

RELIGION

In Ireland, the institutions of health and education are infused with religion. The Church has historically been a key provider of both education and health to the Irish nation, and there may have been benefits to this in the past.[31] The NHE found that stronger religious belief (though we did not ask about institutional religious practice) was weakly, but positively, associated with greater happiness.

In a modern and more inclusive Ireland it is important that our schools reflect our lives and that the state financially supports schools that are practically and symbolically open to all, including all faiths. This is not to deny the right of any religious group to establish their own schools (and hospitals), but national resources need to reflect national values and systems, and be seen to be inclusive of all.

Health and education are just two examples, but poignant ones, where the 'rubber hits the road' when it comes to fairness. In neither case do we take issue with any individual's or group's 'right to choose', but rather with the ultimate symbolism and indeed the ineffectiveness of such unfair systems. What does our healthcare system say about us as a nation, about our values and how we value others? Wouldn't it indeed be ironic if the very inequalities of our healthcare system were among the factors contributing to poorer health and less happiness in the country?

COMMUNITY

Community is one of those topics that can fall into the trap of misguided sentimentality and nostalgic wishing for a country that no longer is (or never was?). However, for us, the value of any real community group or activity lies in the proven link with increasing and sustaining our mutual happiness by deepening our relationships and increasing our own happiness.[32] Historically in Ireland the parish and the pub have been central to bringing people together and they have been complemented by various sporting and hobbyist groups – from golf clubs to book clubs.

Arguably, one of the most important outlets for community in Ireland has been the Gaelic Athletic Association – the GAA – the largest sporting organisation in Ireland with more than 800,000 members. Interestingly, the 'fair play' ethos at the heart of the GAA traces its inspiration back to the equitable ethos of the mythical Celtic warriors – Na Fianna. The GAA has a strict emphasis on amateurism and provides both a health-promoting focus for young people to engage in sport and a common goal for their die-hard supporters, many living perpetually in the hope of the Saw Doctors anthem, 'To Win Just Once'.

It is possible that emerging Irish communities will be built around common purposes that become relevant in these austere times. Initiatives like the Clonakilty Favour Exchange[33] have been set up as a skills and labour exchange, based on an 'economy of goodwill' rather than money. Scarce resources in the workplace and across broader society have inspired organisations like DCU, Trinity and Ulster Bank to set up (unpaid) Mentoring Schemes,[34] instead of over-reliance on paid coaches and consultants. Inability to 'trade up' in property may mean that urban neighbours come together to host street parties and create community gardens. The role of government in this context becomes one of facilitator, not dictator – to help spread ideas, promote networks and provide support.

Our results on optimism – both personal and national – are very encouraging and this 'social capital', this 'fuel for the future', needs to be facilitated by community as well as country-wide initiatives that take advantage of our propensity to volunteer, and our optimism that we will do good deeds for others, as shown in the NHE. To paraphrase Jane Jacobs' wise words about cities, 'Communities have the capability of providing something for everybody, only because and only when, they are created by everybody'.[35] Volunteering should not be taken as an easy way of replacing jobs as a source of meaning and purpose in life. As we noted in Chapter 1, a job, including part-time working, seems to be strongly associated with well-being.

IDENTITY

We found that people who were proud to be Irish and proud to be European were happier and more satisfied than average. Our participants also strongly felt that Ireland had a unique and valuable identity (averaging 7.5 out of 10). On their own, these findings are highly encouraging – but it does make us wonder how can we pin down this identity and harness it to deliver more happiness for ourselves at home as well as the world? In international research[36] comparing the relative strength of different countries as 'brands', Ireland scored in the top twenty which is a great achievement, considering our small size. It may well be asked, apart from our beautiful landscape and gregarious people, what is Ireland's unique value, at home as well as abroad? Next year Ireland will host 'The Gathering – Ireland 2013', a series of events and festivals to celebrate Irish culture, history and genealogy – a year-long country-wide public celebration of 'being Irish'.[37] However, when New Year's Day 2014 dawns, what changes will we see? What are the new goals that we might set? What are the new actions that we might take? We should not be tied to traditional culture as a historical artefact, but embrace our existing values to forge new pathways and opportunities.

Aristotle succinctly made the link between identity and behaviour when he said, 'We are what we repeatedly do'. Bord Bia – the Irish food board – has recently outlined a clear vision to be a world leader in sustainable food and drink, proven by independently audited sustainability programmes.[38] In what other areas can we lead the world with our behaviour? In what other areas can we lead ourselves to Greater Happiness? Seamus Heaney has exhorted us that 'whatever is given can always be re-imagined'.[39] Can we do this? Can we re-imagine Ireland as a more equitable and happier place that is run 'as if people mattered'?

Performance

In addition to the results from the NHE, we want to briefly link the idea of identity with anticipated work performance: what effects do large pay discrepancies have on work performance? Other research on salary ranges – looking at international aid where expatriate and local workers often can get massively different salaries for doing very similar jobs[7] – has shown large salary discrepancies to be very de-motivating because they are considered unjust. But what about within Ireland where there are some very large salary ranges, for instance in the health sector? We presented our Irish participants with a variety of imaginary scenarios of how pay inequality might affect people's motivation to be *productive* at work, to have *pride* in their country, and their desire to actively *participate* in their country. For each of these dimensions, people's motivation was significantly diminished by the sense of working in a country where pay differences were unfair.[40] These results link nicely to those above; performance and perceptions of fairness are linked.

AGE

The NHE has demonstrated quite a striking age-related effect for both happiness and life satisfaction. Clearly some are less happy than others, and those least happy tend to be between the ages of 20-50. This is perhaps the age range that society as a whole relies most upon to make society work – to secure income, to bring up families, to contribute to community sports, and so on. If this is an 'age of burden' then we have to try to ensure that the burden is equally shared. We often think of supports for the young or the elderly, neglecting the fact that those in between appear to be more burdened. This sector of society needs to be more strongly supported by society in general.

CONCLUSION

Despite the very many intriguing results from the NHE, we have sought to try to restrict ourselves to using the results to comment on some of the difficult policy issues facing government and society at large. We are keen to point out that we are not arguing for a particular 'party political' line; rather, we are giving our interpretation of the implications of some of the results. We do, however, realise that our interpretations are politically resonant. Indeed, if politics is at least in part about the allocation of power and resources – about who gets what – it would be naive to think that such factors wouldn't influence how happy and satisfied people feel. Our results – and those of many other studies – show that they clearly do. The question of course is, what should we do about it? Before making some recommendations, we turn to what individuals can do to cultivate their own happiness.

Chapter 5

WHAT CAN YOU DO?

In the previous chapter we outlined some of the so-cietal implications that arise from the results of the National Happiness Experiment. Many of these require a coordinated policy response, often on the part of government. Yet there are also things that individuals can do to influence their own, and perhaps also other people's, happiness. So in this chapter we describe a few specific actions that you can take by yourself, and where there is a good evidence-base testifying to their effectiveness.

THREE GOOD THINGS

One of the best known exercises asks people to each night write down three good things that happened to them that day, as well as their explanation for why they happened. This could be done for a period of several days to several weeks. One research study[41] which asked people to do this every night for one week found that, compared to a control group, those who recorded three good things every night for a week were significantly happier, and less depressed, even three months later.

While in the NHE we did ask people about the number of positive things that had happened to them, there was no relationship between that number (or the ratio of positive to negative things) and how happy they rated themselves. However, our rating was a 'once-off' rating and it is likely that the repeated nightly recoding of three positive things has a cumulative effect, perhaps mediated by increasing people's attention to positive things happening in their life across several consecutive days. So, don't let our 'once-off' rating results put you off – try this simple task for yourself and test out whether it's beneficial or not.

OPTIMISING OPTIMISM

There are a variety of exercises that encourage people to think about a good future. For instance, in one study[42] participants envisaged a positive future in various facets of their life (relationships, friends, family, work) some time between 1-10 years in the future. They wrote, as vividly as possible, about these things and how they had resolved some of their existing problems by that future date. They were also asked to convey sage advice from this future self to the person they are now. This they did each day for one week. Compared to a control condition this exercise was found to increase happiness from the week following the intervention right up to the end of the study six months later; it also decreased feelings of depression for up to three months later in their sample of people prone to depression.

In the NHE we noted that people's average ratings for optimism were actually reasonably high, and higher for 'self' than for 'Ireland'. It might be worth trying to envisage an ideal situation some years ahead for each of these, so that 'my' optimism ratings as well as 'my country's' optimism ratings can support each other's relationship with well-being.

GRATITUDE VISIT

In the NHE we found that people were quite positive about their intention to do good deeds for others, and these intentions were associated with greater happiness; however, the number of good deeds actually done was not associated with happiness. It would be good – wouldn't it - to move the best of intentions into actions?

One study gave participants one week to write and to deliver – in person – a letter of gratitude to someone who had been especially kind to them, but whom they had never really adequately thanked. Compared to a control group, those who completed this task reported an immediate improvement in their happiness, and this increased happiness persisted for one month afterwards. We seem to get a boost by giving due recognition to the kindness of others, so perhaps this is also related to the sense of justice and fairness that we noted as being problematic in Ireland.

RANDOM ACTS OF KINDNESS

This is one of the positive psychology interventions which, rather than being targeted hedonistically at the self, is actually targeted at others. Random acts of kindness are simply things you do for other people without wishing for or anticipating any benefit accruing to yourself, or expecting it to be reciprocated. For instance, one now 'iconic' example is paying for the car that comes behind you at the motorway toll, even though you have no idea who may be in that car. However, doing the wash-up for a flatmate or carrying someone's shopping to their car – basically, putting yourself out for others, all qualify as random acts of kindness. Interestingly, it seems that the benefits of these acts are greatest if, say, five acts of kindness are done all within one day, rather than say doing one a day over a week. In the first case you are more likely to get a positive reaction to your kindness if you have several goes in one day, while if you do it one day after another the novelty will wear off and it might even become a bit of a chore! These positive acts of kindness toward others are thought to bolster self-regard, facilitate positive social interactions and encourage charitable feelings towards others, and, as such, can also be personally beneficial.[43] Remember also the research we described in Chapter 1 illustrating how people feel better about doing things for other people than they do about doing things for themselves – like shopping.

SIGNATURE STRENGTHS

The idea of 'signature strengths' is that there are a range of things that everybody has some strengths in, and it is important to identify and then use them. Following an extensive literature review,[44] a series of 24 character strengths were identified and grouped into six broad virtues. These virtues are wisdom and knowledge (for example, including strengths of having curiosity and a love of learning), courage (for example, including strengths of valour and integrity), love (for example, including strengths of nurturance and emotional intelligence), justice (for example, including strengths of leadership and citizenship), temperance (for example, including strengths of forgiveness and prudence) and transcendence (for example, including strengths of spirituality and appreciation of beauty). These 'strengths' are not therefore 'achievements' or things that you have 'acquired'. Instead, they are personal characteristics or propensities to respond to situations in a certain way.

Luckily, it's easy enough to identify your own strengths, as you can simply go on-line to the 'Values in Action Inventory of Strengths' website,[45] complete the questionnaire – for free – and have your relative strengths profiled for you. This 'Classification of Strengths and Virtues' is a response to the classification systems that psychologists and psychiatrists use to identify what it 'wrong' or problematic for people; except here we are talking about what is 'right' or good about people. It is perhaps surprising that it has taken so long to develop this approach on a scientific basis.[45]

Recent research has suggested that even recognising that you have a range of strengths – by completing the above questionnaire – can have a self-affirming effect, such that individuals who endorsed many character strengths were more likely to report also experiencing a greater sense of meaning in life (assessed by a subsequent question).[46] However, the actual application of strengths seems to reduce stress, increase self-esteem and a sense of vitality (for example, 'I feel alive and vital') even up to six months later.[47] At work, the self-reported opportunity to use perceived strengths is associated with greater well-being and job satisfaction; and in young people aged 12-15, a programme that helped students to identify and use their strengths was found to significantly improve their life satisfaction.[48]

It seems that identifying and using character strengths is a tangible and effective way to enhance well-being. It is, however, important to point out that strengths are not necessarily just 'sitting there' waiting to be used; they may be dormant, but they can also be developed and strengthened. Thus, even if a particular strength is not something you currently possess, it doesn't mean that you can't develop it: *strengths can be cultivated.*

LIVING POSITIVE PSYCHOLOGY

The specific mechanisms through which 'positive psychology exercises' work, and the extent to which they are beneficial for increasing positive states (for example, happiness, life satisfaction, well-being) as well as reducing negative states (such as depression) remain a topic of debate and current research.[49] It is however clear that these exercises can indeed make a strong positive contribution to individuals' real lives,[50] can be used with groups, and are applicable in schools as well as work settings.

There is of course no one magic bullet for happiness or life satisfaction; rather, it is about patterning your life in such a way to engage more with things that are more likely to make you happy. UCD's Professor Alan Carr, in his excellent textbook *Positive Psychology: The Science of Happiness and Human Strengths,*[51] suggests three key components to this patterning. The first one is about human relationships, the need to cultivate relationships that create deep attachments and commitment, psychologically investing yourself in others and repay others' investment in you – 'having someone's back', and knowing they have yours, is self-affirming and strengthening.

The second component is absorbing yourself in work and/or leisure which allows you to use your strengths, talents and interests. Find something that enthrals you, and make the time to lose yourself in it, give yourself space, get 'locked-on' to your passion. And don't worry if others think you are a 'nerd', an 'anorak', a 'space cadet' – their bemusement can be your amusement!

The third component is about nurturing optimism. Dare to imagine yourself and a future where things work out for the best, where you are able to have the right things in the right places. Optimism cultivates good things, it prepares you for them, making it more likely that you can create the situations you want and/ or are better able to exploit them when they come along. The self-protection of pessimism – if I don't expect it I can't be hurt – is a losing game that you talk yourself into, and then walk yourself into.

Having considered some of the things that 'we' as a society can collectively do to create the conditions that are more likely to promote happiness for most people, and then some of the things that we can do as individuals for ourselves, we conclude by pin-pointing a few specific actions in the final chapter.

Chapter 6

NEXT STEPS TOWARDS HAPPINESS

It will probably be quite obvious what some of the implications of the ideas discussed in this book are. However, we want to conclude by making a few simple and concrete suggestions which we hope will stimulate further discussion and action to promote greater happiness and life satisfaction in Ireland.

Our suggestions are relevant not only to promoting happiness, but also to countering despair. While happiness and sadness, elation and depression, satisfaction and despair, may be at opposites ends of a range of related spectra, the same factors may affect them. For instance, as you may have noted in the previous chapter, some of the exercises that have been shown to increase happiness have also been demonstrated to reduce depression, even depression of clinical severity. Many people are affected by and worried about depression and increasing rates of suicide which are so often an enactment of despair and hopelessness. If it can be argued that how our society functions can actually cultivate despair and suicide,[52] then surely it can also be argued that society should be designed to cultivate happiness and life satisfaction. Society should be, can be – must be! – designed to promote a general sense of well-being for the maximum proportion of its participants.

In doing so – in our relationships, in our play, in our work, in our schools and in some of the key institutions of our society – we can both increase the well-being of those 'muddling through' and perhaps decrease the despair of those who are really struggling. However, it is also important to recognise that 'positive psychology'[53] does not set out to eradicate painful emotions which are often an entirely appropriate response to the reality of people's lives, and as such an integral part of the human experience. So while, for instance, loss of a loved one or a personal injury are necessarily difficult experiences about which it is appropriate to feel bad, at the same time navigating these painful emotions can contribute to greater happiness and indeed re-evaluation of one's life.

Below then are just a few next steps we can take that might lead us to the sort of Ireland that we would want to live in. These are all things we can do if we want to live in a society where people – above all else – are what matter to us. These ideas chime with a 'reset' rather than a 're-start' philosophy, and as such are likely to rankle some who want to 'get back' to where we were. Rather than rethink, avoid 'wasting a good crisis' and move forward in a new direction. Several of these recommendations are 'hot' issues in current debates, but perhaps their contribution to happiness, satisfaction and well-being have not been sufficiently appreciated.

1. **Don't be complacent.** We should not take the relatively high ratings that Ireland has on measures of happiness and satisfaction as a reason to avoid taking measures that, according to available evidence, have a good chance of increasing the nation's happiness.

2. **Encourage inclusive education.** Schooling should be multi-denominational (all religions) and co-educational (girls and boys together); it should include marginalised groups, such as people with disabilities and Travellers. Religion should be a central aspect of community life for those who want it, but its rites of passage should not structure the school day or calendar.

3. **Fund schools that promote equal access for all.** The perception that education is equally available to all is a crucial element in developing a national psyche and expectation of social justice – that people will be treated fairly. Access for all

schooling should be targeted to become a signature strength of Irish society.

4. **Develop a healthcare system that allows equal access to all and prioritisation on the basis of healthcare needs.** We need to avoid mixing priority with privatised privilege – both for human rights and social justice reasons – as healthcare is another signature institution for social justice.

5. **Provide more support for the 20s-50s.** While we (rightly) provide social supports for those who are younger and older, we provide little support for those who undertake much of the work in our society, earn much of the income and are the least happy and satisfied. Government-funded pre-school care may be one way of doing this; there are likely many others. Unless we can keep this productive sector of our society on these shores, we will all be much worse off for many different reasons – family and community, social and economic.

6. **Establish a National Taskforce.** We should, like other countries, afford happiness and life satisfaction a much higher priority in our planning and create a mindset that frames our national policies in terms of their contribution to our nation's well-being. This might be facilitated by a 'National

Well-Being Taskforce' who could instigate positive interventions to boost national well-being. Participants in this task force should come from a cross-section of society, including members of marginalised groups.

7. **Establish a National Survey.** There is an old adage that 'what gets measured, gets done'. Robert Kennedy once criticised the idea of GNP (Gross National Product), suggesting that governments measure everything except what makes life worth living. We need a frequent national survey of happiness, satisfaction and well-being, their determinants and indicators. This sort of information can help the government to understand which sort of projects make a positive contribution to people's quality of life and which don't. We need something much larger than the NHE, but perhaps also incorporating its reach and 'easy to respond to' texting method that allows us to sample across time, as events happen, rather than just at set intervals. Such a methodology could help carve out a distinctive approach to happiness in Ireland, and a distinctive contribution to this area of research and social development world-wide.

We realise that these suggestions may be somewhat obvious, but we believe that they make sense, and that they are supported not only by international research and the NHE, but also by an intuitive understanding of the sort of actions that would contribute to a happier nation.

We end with that old joke about psychologists and change:

> *Question*: 'How many psychologists does it take to change a light bulb?'
>
> *Answer*: 'Only one, but the light bulb has to want to change!'

Greater happiness, life satisfaction and well-being are attainable, but we need to be prepared to make the sort of changes that are most likely to secure them.

Appendix One

HOW IRELAND'S HAPPINESS COMPARES TO THE WORLD

To put Ireland's ratings of happiness and satisfaction in international context we briefly review how they compare to other results reported in the *World Happiness Report* (2001), which draws on a large number of different surveys completed over recent years. These surveys are generally of a very large scale (but not across consecutive weeks as ours was), some being census data, and are available for most countries in the world.

Ireland does quite well on such measures when compared to other countries. For instance, on the Cantril Ladder (Worst Possible Life ... to ... Best Possible Life), Ireland is tenth best in the world. Denmark, Finland and Norway come out top, the United States is one below us, and our nearest neighbour, the UK, is eighteenth. Togo, Benin and the Central African

Republic come out worst, with people's ratings there being about less than half those in Ireland.

In terms of Life Satisfaction ratings from the Gallup World Poll (2007-2010), Ireland is placed third, only bettered by Denmark and Costa Rica at the top; the United States is in tenth place and the UK twenty-forth. Tanzania is bottom, with Togo and then Zimbabwe preceding it. Again, the ratings of life satisfaction in these low-income countries is about half that of those in high-income countries. Looking just within Europe, using the results from the latest European Social Survey, Average Life Satisfaction ratings place Ireland tenth out of twenty-four, ahead of the European economic powerhouses (UK, Germany, France) but behind, in particular, the Nordic countries.

So you may be getting the sense that Ireland does pretty well on these measures, but a lot depends on the questions you ask – indeed, a lot depends on the exact phrasing of the questions. So here are some questions that Ireland really likes! For the World Gallup Poll's (2008-2011) question, 'How happy were you yesterday?', top of the world, gold medal position, goes to Ireland, followed by Thailand and New Zealand, whereas yesterday wasn't so good for folk in – you've guessed it – Togo, preceded by Congo and Lithuania. In fact, while over 90 per cent of people in Ireland felt they were happy yesterday, less than 25 per cent of people in Togo felt the same. But, strangely, Denmark (which did so well in terms of Life Satisfaction) comes quite far down the 'Happiness Yesterday' table; in fact, it's at 100, with just over 60 per cent saying they felt happy yesterday.

Finally, the World Gallup Poll's (2005-2011) measure of positive affect (enjoyment, happiness, laughter) gives us a very pleasing shiny Silver, second place medal, just behind Iceland. Iceland? What's that joke about the difference between Iceland and Ireland being one letter and six months? It seems even during the period of economic crisis (which these results span), we might do well, or at least have a good laugh, by keeping each other's company! By the way, Costa Rica was third from the top, US tenth, UK fifteenth, and the other Nordic countries all below us, and Denmark, Germany, and France below them. At the very bottom is Georgia, preceded by Congo and, of course, Togo, again with about half the ratings of the top scoring countries.

So while responses to different questions do differ, the overall patterns of responses, at least at the extremes (top and bottom) of the tables, tends to be (but are not always) similar. It is not just rich countries that do well, poorer ones can do well too, but the ones that do least well tend to be blighted by extreme poverty and/or civil unrest. The good news for us is that Ireland tends to do fairly well across a number of different types of ratings, with our levity and recall of yesterday being exceptionally good – the *craic* was mighty! So we are relatively happy, and this could be a great natural national resource – how then can we strengthen it, nurture it and use it to best effect?

Appendix Two

SOME QUESTIONS FROM THE NATIONAL HAPPINESS EXPERIMENT

You could answer these before reading Chapter 2 and then compare you own answers with the people who participated.

On a scale from 1-10, where 1 = not at all, and 10 = very much, just write beside the question a number that indicates:

1. How happy do you feel now?

2. How satisfied with life in general you feel?

3. How religious would you say you are?

4. How healthy do you feel?

5. In general, do you feel that Ireland is a fair place?

6. In general, do you feel that powerful people are kept in check by media, law and public opinion?

7. In general, do you feel that Ireland has a unique and valuable identity?

8. How proud to be Irish do you feel?

9. How proud to be European do you feel?

10. How many positive things have happened to you in the last 24 hours?

11. How many negative things have happened to you in the last 24 hours?

12. These days you can be contacted most times of the day and night, how good does this make you feel?

13. These days you can contact other people most times of the day and night, how good does this make you feel?

14. Have you done a kind deed for someone in the last week? If so, how many kind deeds?

15. Has anyone done a kind deed for you in the last week? If so, how many kind deeds?

16. How likely would you be to do a kind deed for somebody in the next week? (back to 1-10 ratings)

17. How likely would you be to ask for help from others if you needed it, in the next week?

18. How optimistic do you feel for your future?

19. How optimistic do you feel for Ireland's future?

Appendix Three

SOME QUOTATIONS FROM PARTICIPANTS IN THE NATIONAL HAPPINESS EXPERIMENT

The 294 people who completed the response for the sixth week also texted in observations when we asked if they wished to make any comment on their experience of participating in the National Happiness Experiment. We are really grateful for this feedback. About 30 per cent of these remarks expressed gratitude for doing the survey and thanking the organisers of it. Approximately another 10 per cent were upset about the National Happiness Experiment website which they had tried to access and had had problems with (sorry again!). Some 10 per cent made comments on the design of the National Happiness Experiment and a further 10 per cent wanted to know whether and when they would get feedback – for the whole survey and individually. We won't give individual feedback but participants may want to use questions in Appendix One to remind them of some of your responses, and hopefully this book will help to place them in a broader context.

Approximately 40 per cent of comments were positive and mentioned specific ways the survey had helped them, or specific events that had happened, during the survey. We reproduce some of these comments below because we found them interesting and, indeed, some of them quite inspiring.

EXAMPLES OF COMMENTS

thanks for the opportunity it was great especially to realise how happy i am hopefully i am not alone

it was a very interesting survey to part take in cant wait to see the results i hope there will be more in the future thank you xxx

doing the survey made me realise how generally happy i am at this point in my life

i really enjoyed the experience even just been asked each week makes me take stock of my life and it ain t so bad

taking part made me focus on all the positives in my life in a time when negativity is almost a national pastime

this experiment really forced me to take an honest look at my life its amazing how a simple question can open your eyes to whats right or wrong in your life

i love my country just the government i hate proud to b irish but fed up been treated like 2nd class citizens

it kept me positive about my life having 2 think about it thanx

i am goin through a rough time at the minute i am usually much happier

hi was a good exercise to question my personal satisfaction levels had 3 major surgeries in 3 weeks and this was very beneficial thank u

it was fun taking part i would do it again made me think of my state of mind

happiness outlook luck we need more happy research these days and less gloom thanks for ur efforts

i enjoyed taking part mainly because it gave me an oppurtunity to realise what is good in my life and what i need to be grateful for annette

i thought it was very interesting and cool

tk u while takin part i became aware that i could still b happy even though going through tough times personaly

thank u it was good 2 stop n think n count my blessings best of luck

it has made me aware of what happiness really is i deliberately do acts of kindness now state of mind is a conscious choice thanks

i really enjoyed d experiment it was a very positive experience

questions were asked at a very turbulent time in my life since i am preparing to leave ireland for greener pastures in the next few months thank you

really made me think i am happier than i though i was even on rainy days

thought provoking questions not too samey a survey of its time qs about religion and future of ireland very apt well done the sg can t wait for results

this experiment made me aware of how many little dramas life throws every week of one s life of how these little things effect daily happiness levels

i do intend to view web v interesting questions make you think deeply afterwards plus discussions raised

ask people wiat weather is like in their localty s the weaver does affect mood enjoyed doing it till again bye

happiness levels change daily depending on what s going on in your life there is no path to happiness happiness is the path siddhartha gautama aka Buddha

i couldn t understand why u kept asking de same questions week after week it made de survey pretty boring

we will only ever b happy in this life by coming to know jesus truly present in theeucharist

thank you i hope to change my life and be happy

do u know any good looking femail between 30 and 40 that might go out with me

isn t this a survey rather than an experiment

well done on this initiative and good luck with your work

thank u

REFERENCES

1. Schumacher E.F. *Small is Beautiful: Economics as if people mattered.* Washington, U.S.: Hartley and Marks Publishers Inc. 1999.

2. Seligman M.E.P. *Authentic Happiness: Using the new positive psychology to realize your potential for lasting fulfillment.* New York: The Free Press; 2002.

3. Froth J.J. Happiness. In: Lopez S.J., ed. *The Encyclopedia of Positive Psychology.* Chichester: Wiley-Blackwell; 2009.

4. Brickman P. and Campbell D.T. Hedonic relativism and planning in the good society. In: Appley MH, ed. *Adaptation Level Theory: A symposium.* New York: Plenum Press; 1971:287-302.

5. Cantril H. *The Pattern of Human Concerns.* New Brunswick, NJ: Rutgers University Press; 1965.

6. Layard R., Clark A. and Senik C. The causes of happiness and misery. In: Helliwell J, Layard R, Sachs J, eds. *World Happiness Report.* New York: The Earth Institute; 2012.

7. MacLachlan M., Carr S.C. and McAuliffe E. *The Aid Triangle: Recognizing the human dynamics of dominance, justice and identity.* London: Zed; 2010.

8. ILO. ILO Declaration on Social Justice for a Fair Globalization Geneva: ILO; 2008.

9. Furnham A. Justice at work. In: Carr S.C., MacLachlan M., Furnham A., eds. *Humanitarian Work Psychology*; 2012.

10. Wilkinson R.G., Pickett K. *The Spirit Level: Why more equal societies almost always do better.* London: Allen Lane; 2009.

11. Helliwell J.F. How's Life? Combining individual and national variables to explain subjective well-being. *Economic Modelling.* 2003; 20:331-360.

12. Knack S. Trust, Associational Life and Economic Performance. In: Helliwell J.F. and Bonikowska A, eds. *The Contribution of Human and Social Capital to Sustained Economic Growth and Well-being.* Ottawa and Paris: Human Resources Development Canada and OECD; 2001:172-202.

13. Stevenson B. and Wolfers J. Happiness Inequality in the United States. *Journal of Legal Studies.* 2008; 37(S2):S33-79.

14. GWP. Gallup World Poll 2005-2011 [the_gallup_071511. dta]: Gallup Inc.; 2011.

15. Anik L., Aknin L.B., Norton M.I. and Dunn E.W. Feeling Good about Giving: The benefits (and costs) of self-interested charitable behavior: Harvard Business School Discussion Paper No. 10-012; 2010.

16. Harbaugh W.T., Mayr U. and Burghart D.R. Neural responses to taxation and voluntary giving reveal motives for charitable donations. *Science.* 2007; 316(5831):1622-1625.

17. Davidson R.J. and Harrington A., eds. *Visions of Compassion: Western Scientists and Tibetan Buddhists Examine Human Nature.* New York: Oxford University Press; 2002.

18. Cohen S., Doyle W.J., Turner R.B., Alper C.M. and Skoner D.P. Emotional style and susceptibility to the common cold. *Psychosomatic Medicine.* 2003; 65:652-657.

19. Steptoe A., Wardle J. and Marmot M. Positive affect and health-related neuroendocrine, cardiovascular, and inflammatory processes. *Proc Natl Acad Sci USA.* 2005; 102(18):6508-6512.

20. Carstensen L.L., Turan B., Scheibe S., *et al.* Emotional Experience Improves with Age: Evidence based on over 10 years of experience sampling. *Psychol Aging.* 2011; 26(1):21-33.

21. MacLachlan M. *Culture and Health.* Chichester: Wiley; 2006.

22. Kahneman D. *Thinking, fast and slow.* London: Penguin; 2011.

23. Blanchflower D.G. and Oswald A.J. Is well-being U-shaped over the life cycle? *Social Science and Medicine.* 2008; 66(8):1733-1749.

24. Seidlitz L. and Diener E. Memory for positive versus negative life events: Theories for the differences between happy and unhappy persons. *J Pers Soc Psychol.* Apr 1993; 64(4):654-664.

25. Schwartz R.M. Consider the simple screw: Cognitive science, quality improvement, and psychotherapy. *J Consult Clin Psychol.* Dec 1997; 65(6):970-983.

26. Wilkinson R.G. *Unhealthy societies: The afflictions of inequality* London: Routledge; 1996.

27. MacLachlan M. and O'Connell M., eds. *Cultivating Pluralism: Psychological, social and cultural perspectives on a changing Ireland.* Dublin: Oak Tree Press; 2000.

28. OECD. Overcoming School Failure - Policies that Work. Ireland: Department of Education, Ireland; 2011.

29. O'Toole F. *Enough is Enough: How to Build a New Republic.* London: Faber and Faber; 2010.

30. OECD Health Data 2012. Available at: http://www.oecd. org/health/healthpoliciesanddata/oecdhealthdata2012.htm. Accessed 01 November 2012.

31. Wren M. *Unhealthy State: Anatomy of a sick society.* Ireland: New Island; 2003.

32. Haidt J. *The Happiness Hypothesis - Putting Ancient Wisdom and Philosophy to the Test of Modern Science.* London: Arrow Books; 2006.

33. Clonakilty Favour Exchange. Available at: http://www. clonfavour.com/. Accessed 01 November 2012.

34. Stanton H. Piloting Mentoring Schemes in Ireland - Talk to the Psychological Society of Ireland. September 2012 ; 2012.

35. Jacobs J. *The Death and Life of Great American Cities.* New York: Vintage Books; 1992.

36. Anholt-GFK Roper National Brand Index - 2012. Brand Ireland should be re-thought and replaced. In: *The Irish Times*: J. Fanning and M. Henry, ed; July 27, 2012.

37. The Gathering Ireland 2013. Available at: http://www. thegatheringireland.com/. Accessed 30 Oct 2012.

38. Bord Bia Irish Food Board. Pathways for Growth: Building Ireland's largest indigenous industry; Year One Progress Update: November; 2010.

39. Heaney S. The Settle Bed. *Seeing Things.* UK: Faber and Faber; 1991:29.

40. Hand K. and MacLachlan M. An unequal balance? The effects of unequal pay systems on societal motivation in Ireland. *Special Edition of the Irish Journal of Psychology.* 2012; 33(2-3):129-136.

41. Seligman M.E., Steen T.A., Park N. and Peterson C. Positive psychology progress: Empirical validation of interventions. *Am Psychol.* Jul-Aug 2005; 60(5):410-421.

42. Shapira L.B. and Mongrain M. The benefits of self-compassion and optimism exercises for individuals vulnerable to depression. *Journal of Positive Psychology.* 2010; 5(5):377-389.

43. Hefferon K. and Boniwell I. *Positive Psychology: Theory, research and applications.* UK: Open University Press; 2011.

44. Peterson C. and Seligman M.E.P. *Character Strengths and Virtues: A Handbook and Classification.* New York: Oxford University Press; 2004.

45. Penn University of Pennsylvania. Authentic Happiness. Available at: http://www.authentichappiness.sas.upenn.edu/ questionnaires.aspx. Accessed 01 November 2012.

46. Littman-Ovadia H. and Steger M. Character strengths and well-being among volunteers and employees: Toward an integrative model. *Journal of Positive Psychology.* 2010;5(6):419-430.

47. Wood A.M., Linley P.A., Maltby J., Kashdan T.B. and Hurling R. Using personal and psychological strengths leads to increases in well-being over time: A longitudinal study and the development of the strengths use questionnaire. *Personality and I Individual Differences.* 2011; 50(1):15-19.

48. Proctor C., Tsukayama E., Wood A.M., Maltby J., Eades J.F. and Linley P.A. Strengths Gym: The impact of a character-strengths based intervention on the life satisfaction and well-being of adolescents *Journal of Positive Psychology.* 2011; 6(5):377-388.

49. Mongrain M. and Anselmo-Mathews T. Do Positive Psychology Exercises Work? A Replication of Seligman et al (2005). *Journal of Clinical Psychology.* 2012; 68:382-389.

[50.] Cohn M.A. and Fredrickson B.L. In search of durable positive psychology interventions: Predictors and consequences of long-term positive behavior change. *J Posit Psychol.* Sep 1 2010; 5(5):355-366.

[51.] Carr A. *Positive Psychology: The Science of Happiness and Human Strengths (2nd Ed).* London: Routledge; 2011.

[52.] Smyth C., MacLachlan M. and Clare A. *Cultivating Suicide? Destruction of Self in a Changing Ireland.* Dublin: The Liffey Press; 2003.

[53.] Ben-Shahar T. *The Pursuit of Perfect* New York: McGrawHill; 2009.

THANKS TO OUR SPONSORS

We would like to thank the following supporters of the National Happiness Experiment

Thanks for celebrating 50 years with the positive psychology of happiness and supporting the National Happiness Experiment.

Thanks for facilitating the link between the Happy? 'Lab in the Gallery' and the National Happiness Experiment.

Thanks for implementing the National Happiness Experiment, providing a living 'in-the-world' platform for research.

Thanks for supporting the vision of the psychology of happiness, both in the 'Lab in the Gallery' and in our 'Lab in the Nation' – the National Happiness Experiment.

Thanks for providing a stimulating environment for us to work in and asking lots of tricky questions!

All ideas expressed in *Happy Nation?* derive from the authors and do not necessarily reflect the views of any of those supporting the National Happiness Experiment.